D1614179

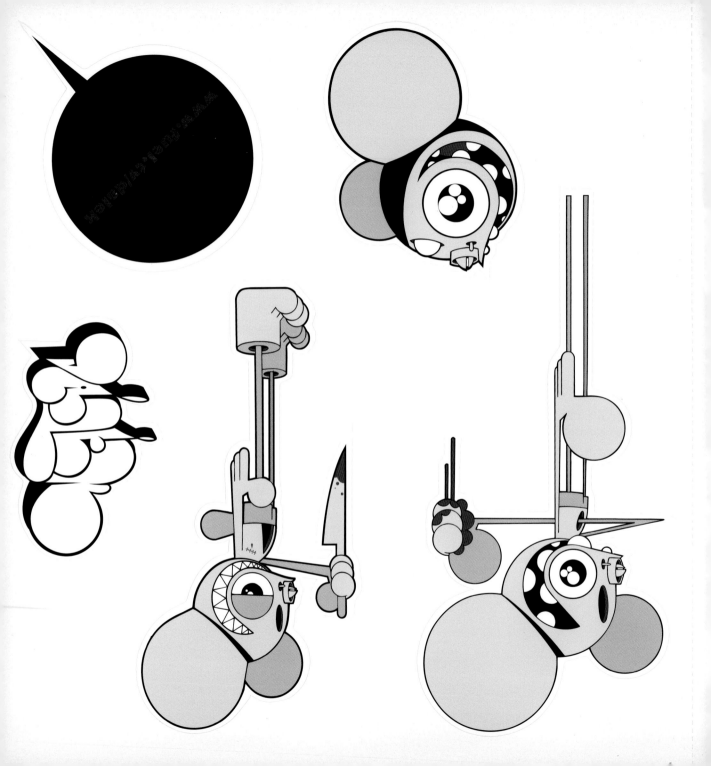

www.dalekart.com

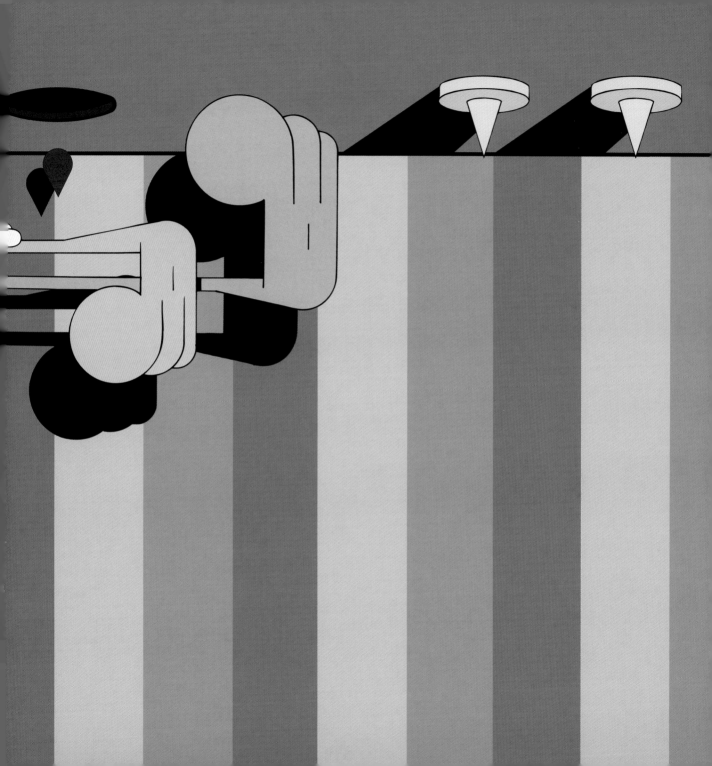

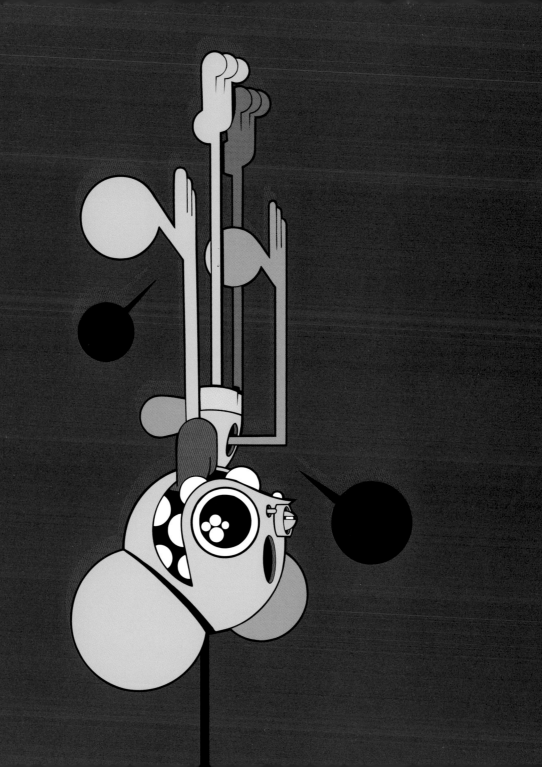

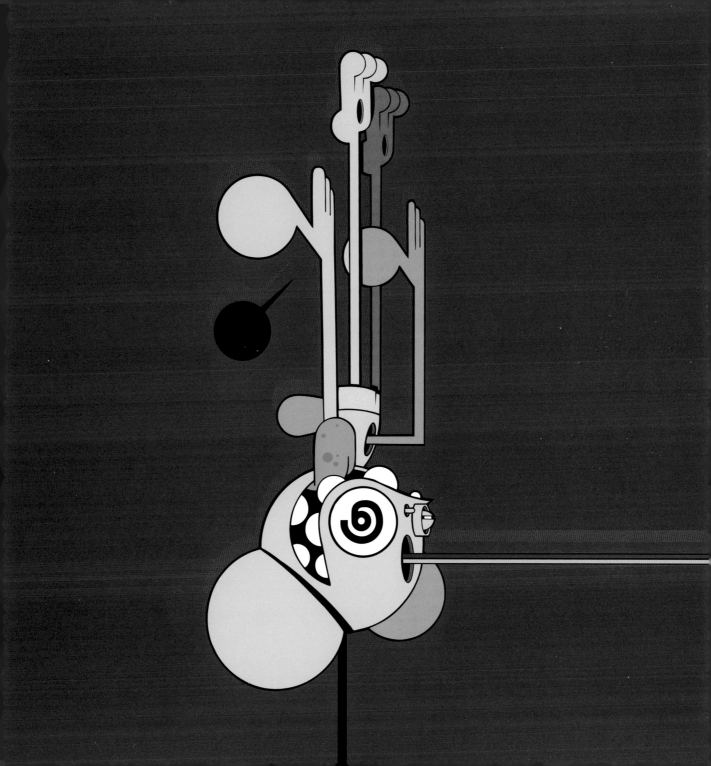

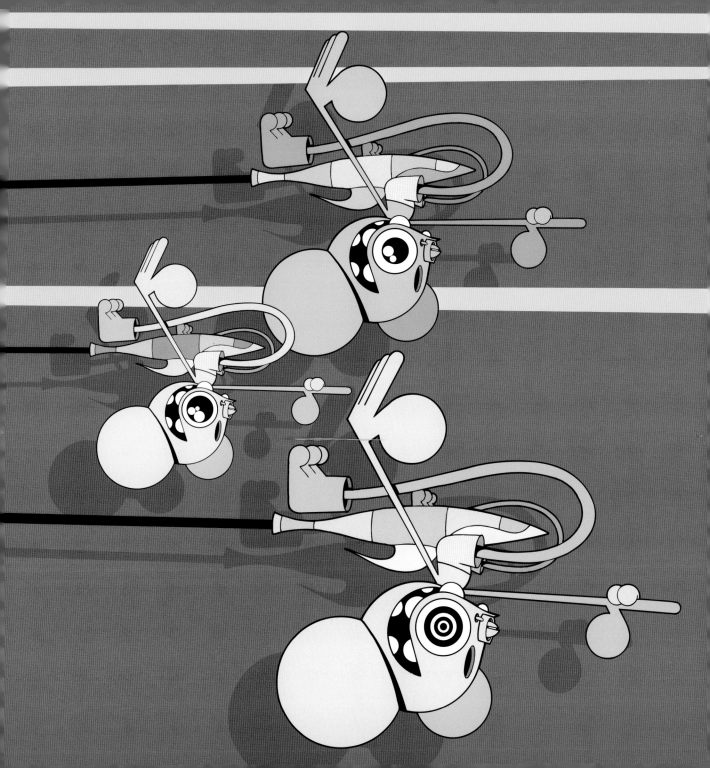

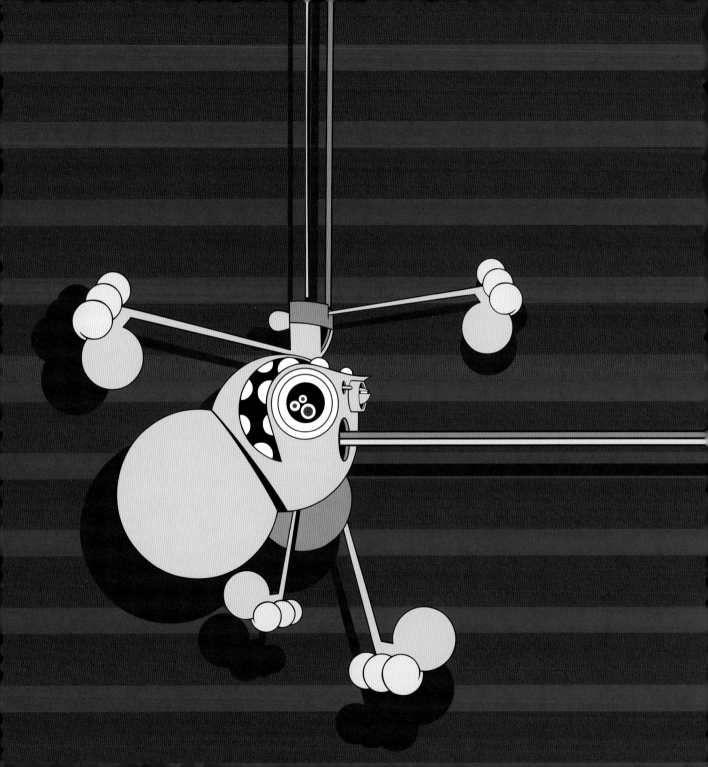

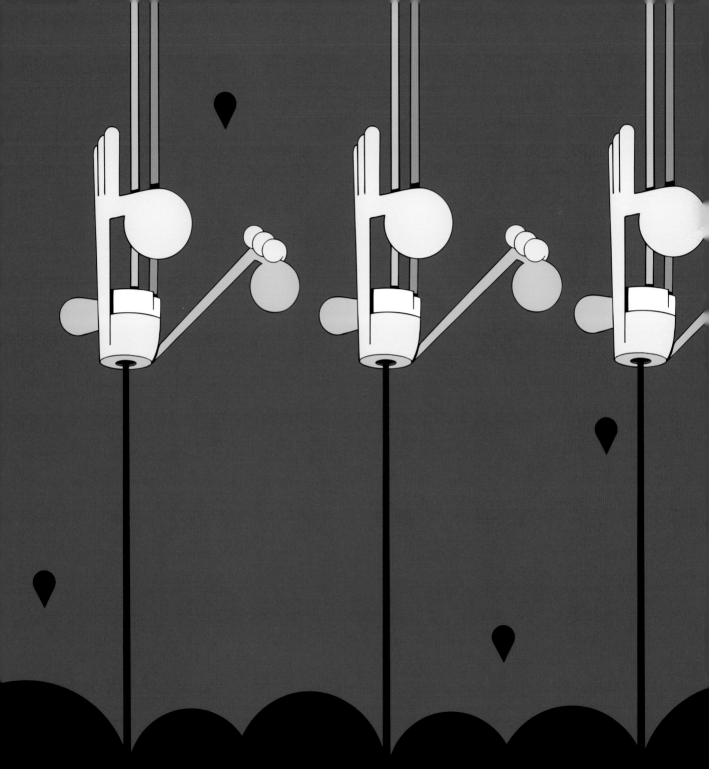

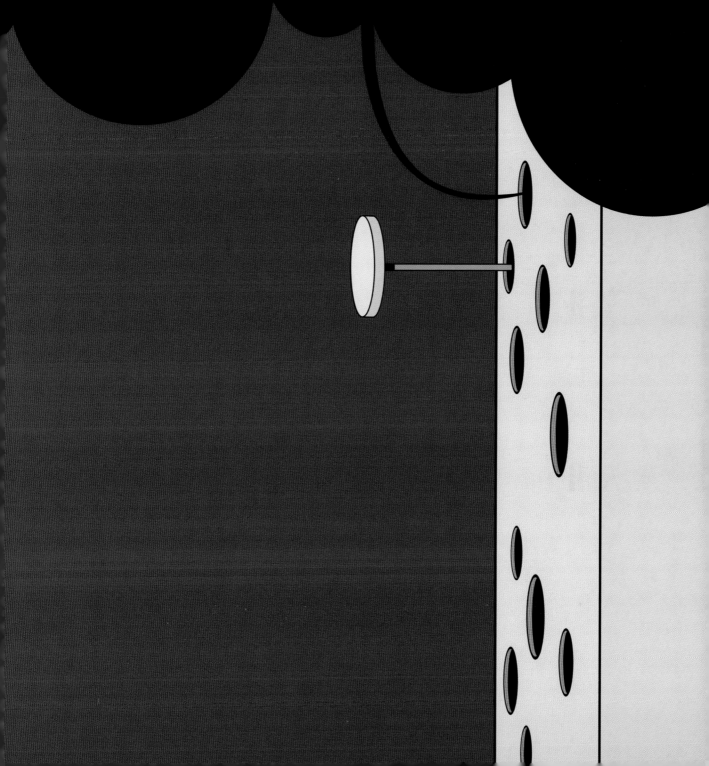

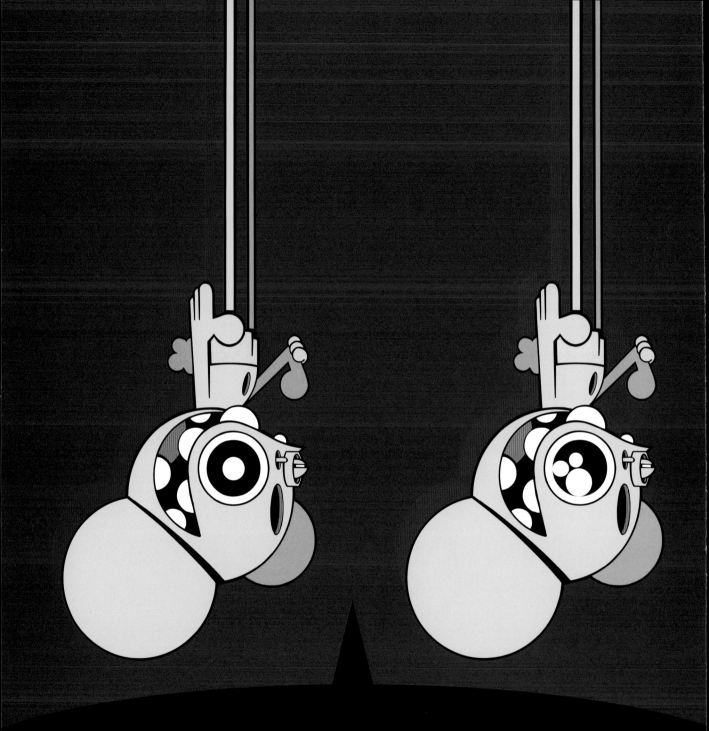

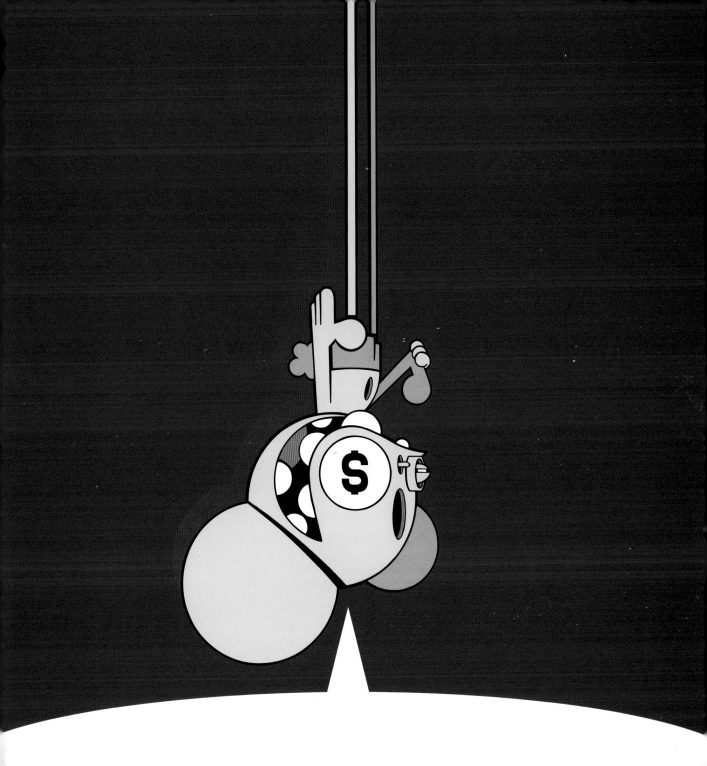

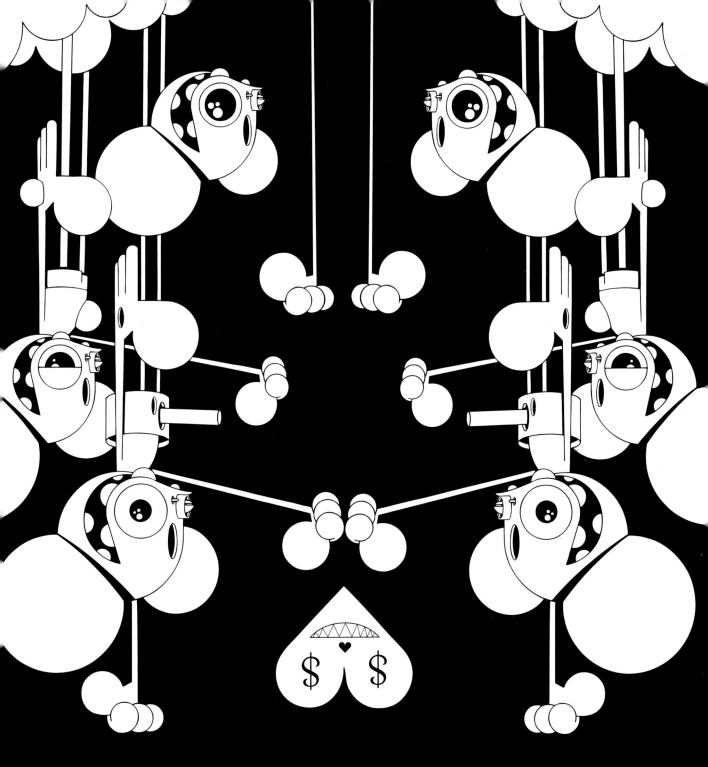

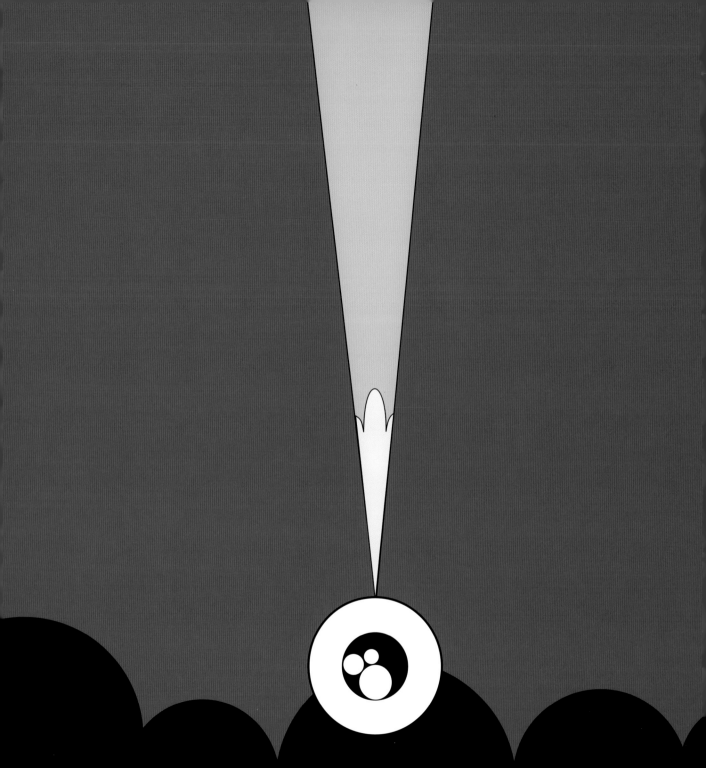

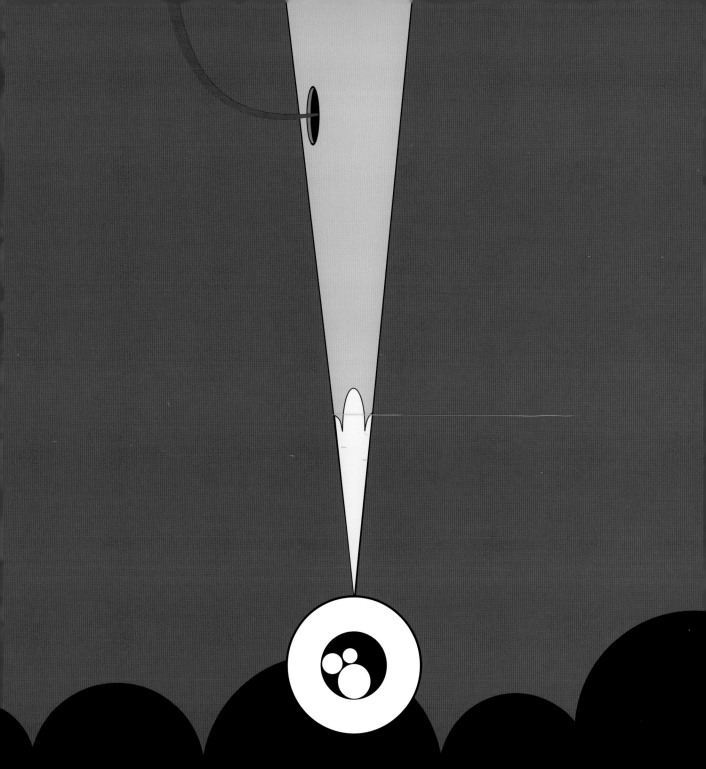

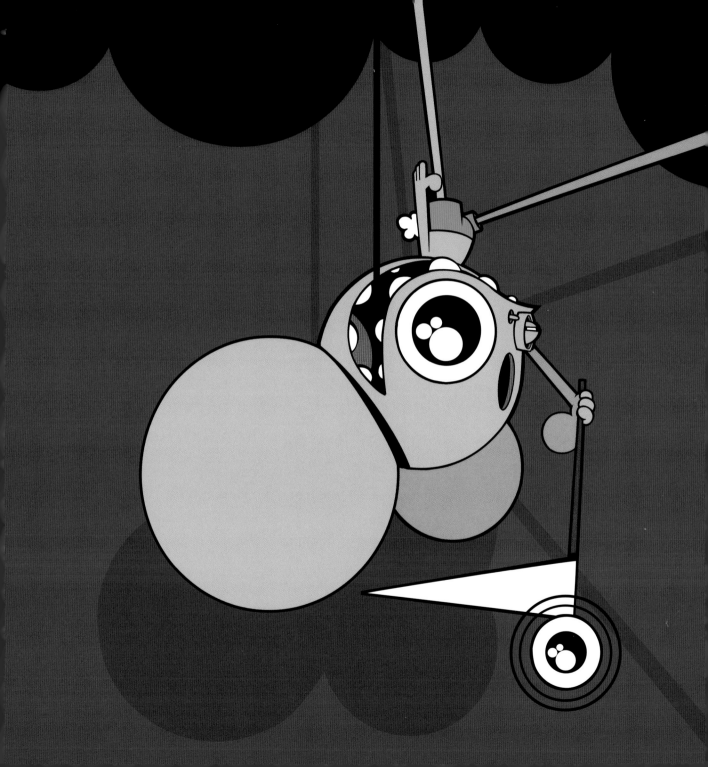

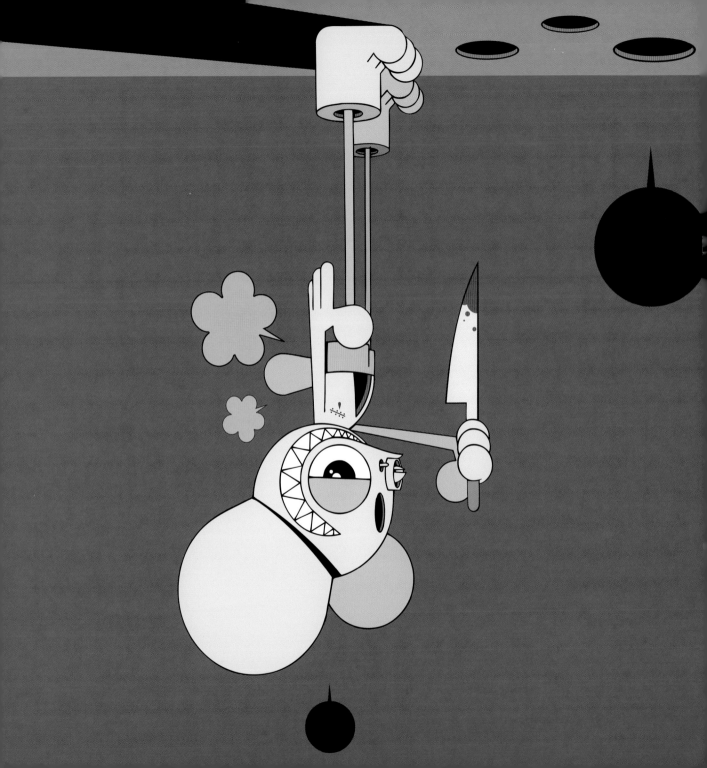

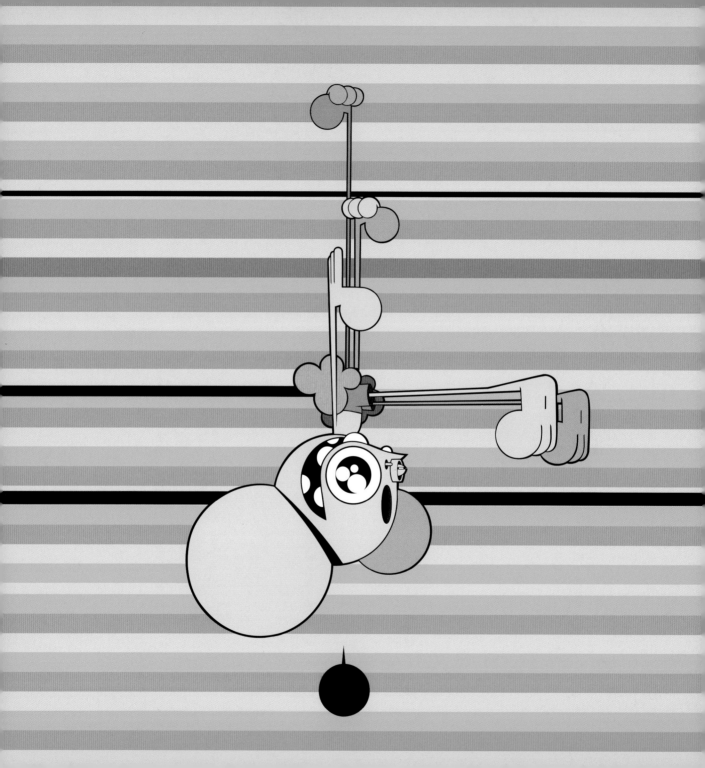

"I am a collector by nature. I have endless amounts of unnecessary objects in my home: skateboards, toys, records, books, shirts, shoes, paint cans… So, to some extent I know that my desire to create product falls in line with my obsession with material possessions."

I can trade toys for other toys; I create for other toys; books for books; prints for prints; I can continue my massive collection."

Assuming the power of production to shape his environment.

Growing up in a world of mass-produced goods.

paintings
drawings
vector
digital
walls

Are we looking at computer files or reproductions of objects? Does it matter?
We no longer live in the age of mechanical reproduction, but the age of digital production.
How to materialize information?

THE WORK CANNOT BE RESTRAINED OR CONTAINED.

"It's also really cool to make objects that are accessible to thousands of people. It is a great way to get art out to people who can't or don't want to buy original paintings."

SUPPLYING THE DEMAND

products

manboytoycollectors

"Products are a great source of bonus income.
In reality, it is not as lucrative as original artwork
and can often be far more time consuming and annoying.
You have to deal with outside folks to get the
job done: samples back and forth…all that crap.
But in seeing the finished product, there is a certain
satisfaction that differs from seeing a painting finished.
Maybe it is the mass of a production run."

drips

drips

s d r i p s

PRODUCTIONS FOR THESE PAGES VS. REPRODUCTIONS ON THESE PAGES VS. REPRODUCTIONS OF THESE PAGES

DRIPS DROP, DROP SHADOWS.

SIGNIFIERS OF PAINTING. IRONIC ICONS OF AN ANTIQUATED PROCESS.

drips

Pictorial depth is a visual joke.

False layers: Representations of stage sets.

ORIFICES : GATEWAYS : PASSAGES : POCKETS

shadows

cast + ing

A DEPTH OF NO FIELD

HOLES

VOIDS : TRAPS : VENTS :

We are caught in the middle.

SECRETS IN THE SHADOWS REVEAL WHAT IS GOING ON BEHIND THE VIEWER

The viewer is the light.

two dimensions?

Why use SHAPE & LINE to define space in

Warp-around.
space.
Wrap-around
or projection.
a flat screen
as opposed to
on the wall
that hangs
at an object
are looking
that we
reminds us
edges
the painting's
Addressing

Outlines: an aesthetic from the animation industry.

Cleaning up butting color blocks.

Cell painting.

HOLES
AND
SMILES
AND
FEET
AND
EARS
AND
DRIPS
AND
POOFS
AND
GROUNDS
AND
CLOUDS

Takashi Murakami high on goofballs.

Always in gravity

HEAVEN SENT

An extension of the self.

SPACE MONKEYS
NASA'S BAKER & ABLE
NEIL ARMSTRONG
STRETCH ARMSTRONG
PLANET OF THE APES

CREATION

A KAWS TAKEN UP BY MANY OF MARSHALL'S PEERS.

CHARACTER

space

flat space

past

onkeys

WHY RIGHT TO LEFT?

LEFT and RIGHT?

There are UPS and DOWNS and

Cartoon Physics

Marshall
does not
(re)present
rendered forms
but flat
tone-on-tone
shapes

I expect
to see
the Creator's eraser
enter the
picture plane
from beyond Flatland
to destroy a
spacemonkey.

DARTOO

DARTOON

Deploying Daleks

EXCEPT "PSYCHO KILLER (QU'EST-CE QUE C'EST)?" WHICH IS THE TITLE OF A TALKING HEADS SONG

The Daleks live in robotic fighting machines.

They say, "Exterminate" and "**I Obey**".

THE DALEKS ARE MUTATIONS OF A HUMANOID SPECIES FROM THE PLANET SKARO.

In the Dr. Who world, the Daleks

were hell-bent on total domination.

They infiltrated our world through

A FAVORITE WORD OF ONE OF MARSHALL'S CONTEMPORARIES: SHEPARD THE SHEPHERD.

merchandising: toys, models,

pajamas, slippers, soap, cereal,...

Each Dalek is expendable for the greater good of their race.

James Marshall, he's my friend

Foreword
BY RYAN McGINNESS

PSYCHO KILLER

(Qu'est-ce que c'est?)

FARTS AND DAGGERS

**They are all self-portraits.
You can see it in the eyes.**

He's been making James Juniors for years.

AND EMPTY SPEECH BUBBLES: SILENT BUT DEADLY

James Marshall worked for Takashi Murakami from October 2001 through March 2002.

"IT WAS A GREAT

EXPERIENCE.

I LEARNED

SO MUCH ABOUT

HIS TECHNIQUE

AND STUDIO

PRACTICES. I ADOPTED

A LOT OF THESE

PRACTICES AND ADAPTED

THEM TO MY OWN

NEEDS.

IT DRAMATICALLY

CHANGED THE WAY

I CREATE ART."

Published in 2005 by R77
© R77, All Rights Reserved

isbn 1-57687-247-5

Compiled and Edited by Roger Gastman
Art Direction by Tony Smyrski (www.crashcontentcreative.com)
Foreword text and design by Ryan McGinness
All artwork by James Marshall/DALEK
Special thanks to Sara Rosen

R77 Publishing
PO Box 34843
Bethesda, Maryland, 20827
USA
info@graffsupply.com

Made possible by FUEL TV
24/7 action sports television
Visit www.fuel.tv/dalek for special goodies from FUEL TV.

Fuel TV logo :
TM & ©2004 FUEL TV, Inc. All Rights Reserved.

First Printing

For more information on DALEK visit www.dalekart.com

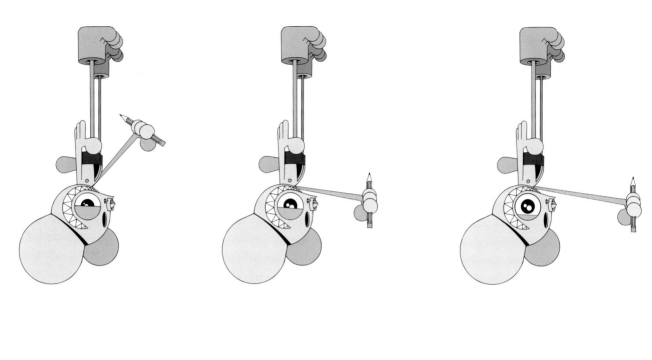

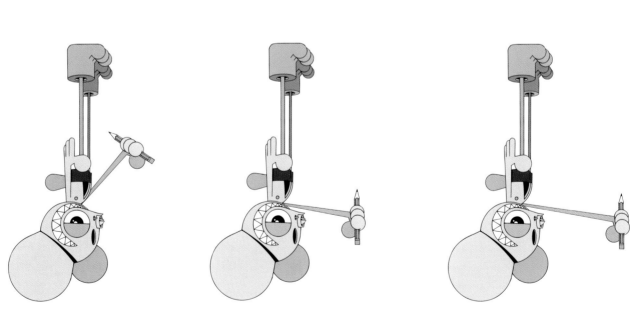

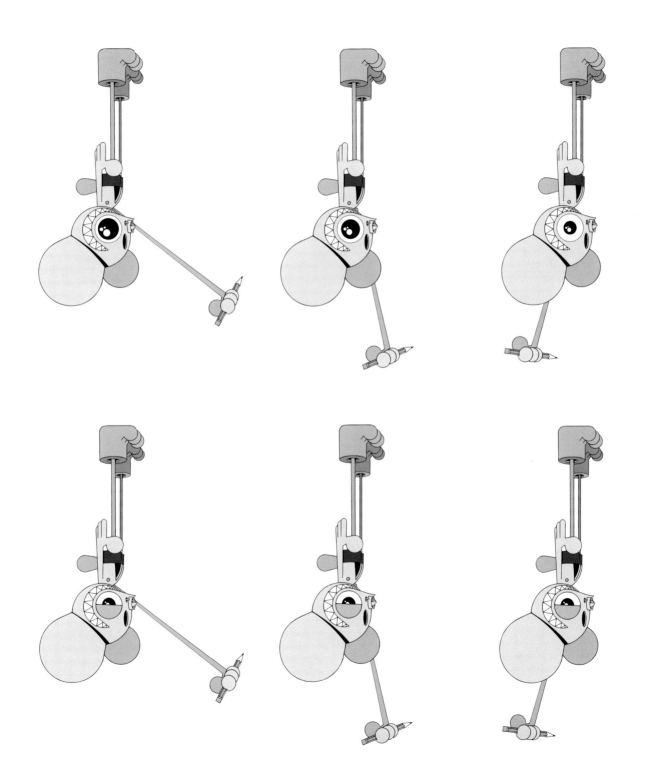